For Dan, and your never-ending support.
Thank you.

" If you always do what you've always done,
you will always get what you've always got. "

Henry Ford

Welcome ♡

Being able to create something new and eye catching from bits and bobs has always made me smile. It's always made my friends and family smile too. There's something very personal and sincere about handmade items, especially when making them for our loved ones.

We live in a disposable world now, and the magic of 'Make, Do and Mend' has been recently reignited into a new generation of upcyclers and salvagers. It's easy to be part of this modern craze. From painting old furniture a new colour, or turning an old frame into a chalkboard in my own experience, the upcycle trend can make you feel like you have achieved something, and that you have put a bit of yourself into your new item. The most exciting part of all of this, is that you can add personality and individuality to an event like a wedding or a birthday, provide you with extra special gifts for friends, or help to turn your house into a home.

My favourite trend to come from this craze is modern signwriting. DIY handwritten signage is growing in popularity, and I would like to share my knowledge and experience of this skill with you.

This guide will help you master the basics of modern signwriting, and allow you to create your own hand lettered signs. You'll be wowing your friends with your makes, turning up to their baby showers and birthdays with amazing, heartfelt decorations – and before long you'll have a list of requests to make more.

Lets get started!

Clair x

CONTENTS

Introduction
A GUIDE TO MODERN SIGNWRITING

Creating handmade items is a rewarding and therapeutic hobby. Keeping our brains and minds active is good for us and makes us feel positive. You also get an amazing feeling of pride when you complete something you have worked hard on.

Running a modern signwriting business is very rewarding, and I feel privileged to be part of some amazing events, weddings, running courses and getting my work published in magazines and books. I'm very fortunate that my hard work has got me to this point. My friends and family were hugely supportive and recognised I was good at creating handmade upcycled pieces, and this led me to creating a real birthday chalkboard for my little girl's first birthday. After setting up The Chalk Spot in 2014 it was apparent that no other business was selling real chalkboards with these personalised designs and that the gap in the market was happy to be filled by a modern signwriting business.

Although sign writing has been around for a long time, with traditional pub signs being the most recognised, it is modern signwriting with elegant handwritten text and simple designs and illustrations that is growing in popularity. There were no guides or tutorials on pinterest when I started so I had to go through months of trial and error, but finally I now have long lasting products, and I am leading the market with fresh designs and ideas. Traditional signwriting will always be an art, a detailed and expert skill that takes natural talent to be good at. Modern signwriting allows everyone an opportunity to create something personal and beautiful.

Personalisation and handlettering is a top trend currently, and there's no better time to learn how to give it a go. Through learning from others during the courses I have taught and from my own experiences, I have been able to put together this guide that will have you creating beautiful handmade signs to be proud of.

Chalkboards

Essential tools and how to make the most from them

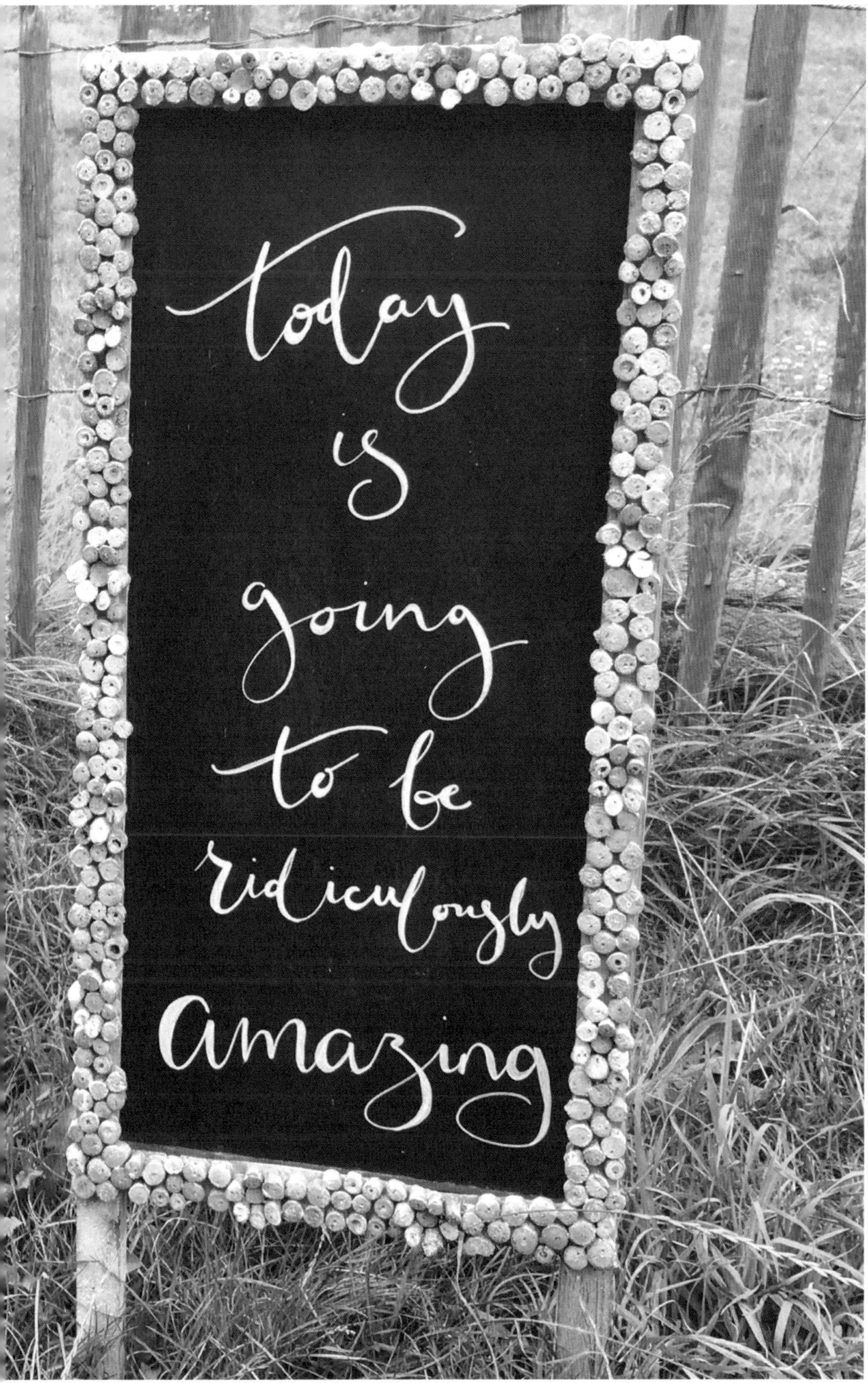
today
is
going
to be
ridiculously
amazing

Mastering Chalkboards

In our guide we are going to learn how to make and decorate a chalkboard first. Chalkboards decorated with artwork and hand lettering are gaining in popularity and are a great place to start. They are the first place I established my own signwriting and they look brilliant when finished.

This chapter will explore the essential tools that i use daily. We will then learn two simple fonts to use on our boards. We shall also discover decorating tips and inspiration, and finally we will bring it all together.

After we have mastered chalkboards, the remaining chapters in this guide will explore different surfaces to apply modern signwriting to.

Starter Kit
FOR
CHALKBOARD SIGNWRITING

The best signwriting equipment is easy to come by. Knowing a couple of my secrets will help your end result become flawless. I recommend starting with these tools. I have chosen items that are easy to buy in most craft and hardware stores. These are the tools I use on my own chalkboards.

PAINT PENS

There's a large range of chalkmarkers on the market used by traditional signwriters and are great for achieving the eye catching graffiti style. Unfortunately, the nibs are fat, the colours are few and far between, and they are not always permanent – most of them can be wiped away.

My preferred materials are the Acrylic based paint pens which are available in a range of sized nibs. These will make your handwriting look elegant and flowing. Posca pens are easy to come by and offer everything a beginner will need.

My preferred nibs

- **PC-3M 1.5MM TIP: perfect for small details such as names on a table plan**
- **PC-5M TIP: perfect for everything else**

THE CHALK SPOT TIP: Start with a white paint pen whilst practicing before expanding your collection to include a range of colours.

✐ PENCIL, ERASER & A RULER

Pencils make easy work for a beginner signwriter. You can sketch your design straight onto your chalkboard and give yourself the opportunity for error before you paint it. Using a very soft lead will not only avoid marking your board with scratches, but will be much easier to rub out. I recommend 5B pencils as they are the softest – don't forget you will need to use a pencil sharpener often as the lead disappears quickly.

Very soft erasers will also avoid leaving any unnecessary marks and smudges.

Always have a ruler handy to pencil lines onto your board if you find it difficult to naturally write in a straight line.

◖ BABY WIPES

Being a mum has taught me baby wipes will save almost any situation, and because they are in large supply in my house, I also discovered they will wipe away any paint mistakes if you are quick enough to get it before the paint dries.

✏ BLACK PAINT PEN OR SHARPIE

It's inevitable that when you are starting out you will make mistakes, or your paint might drip (which can happen if it is warm) If you can't save a mistake with a baby wipe, then the magic of a hand painted chalkboard is you can cover the mistakes up with black paint, or a black sharpie.

🖌 VARNISH

Not all the acrylic paints will survive against the elements; I now use an outdoor proof paint, but when you're getting started there is a simple solution. You can protect the paint on your boards to be weatherproof. This is ideal for boards you might use at a wedding, where you might want to display them outside. To do this you will need a varnish spray paint. These are readily available, and I advise you choose one that is friendly to acrylic paints so they wont make your hard work bleed as soon as you spray it.

If you want to protect the wood board as well to be fully weather proof and keep outside, you will need to treat the wood first with a varnish ideal for outdoors, and then treat your painting on top when you have finished your design, again with a varnish that will not react to the acrylic paint.

MAKING A
Chalkboard

MDF is my favourite wood base for a chalkboard. You can find MDF in most good hardware and DIY stores. If you're really lucky the store might offer a cutting service and you can have your pieces cut to size while you are there.

Chalkboard spray paint is then easy to apply, or chalkboard paint with a large foam brush will have just as great an effect.

BUDGET FRIENDLY

However, you don't have to make your chalkboard just from wood. If you fancy a budget friendly option you can pick up foam boards from good stationers and craft stores, and the acrylic paint pens will work just as well on these also. The benefits are they are lighter and easier to frame. If your budget is even tighter, a thick black card will work just as well.

Please try to avoid buying cheaper 'ready made' chalkboards as they are usually made from synthetic materials and have a smooth surface. The acrylic paint pens will not stay on these boards like they do on a handmade wood chalkboard. Making your own can be just as cheap if you try some of the options mentioned above.

> **THE CHALK SPOT TIP**: Turn to page 64 to discover how to frame a chalkboard.

HOW TO USE
Acrylic PAINT PENS

The paint pens are generally easy to use, and with a little love and care should last you a long time. Remember to shake your pens often to mix up the water based paint (do this with the lid on so the paint doesn't splatter on your board). Pump the nib to fill with paint. Do this onto a scrap piece of paper to avoid any excess paint running onto your board. I always keep a piece of scrap paper handy for prepping my pens after every break.

When you start your design always be aware of your hand, and work from top to bottom – I have learnt frequently that its very easy to smudge your design with your hand. Allow your design time to dry as you work on it.

DRAWING ON YOUR CHALKBOARD

Start by making sure your board is clean and dry. Any dust or debris on the board will eventually wear down your nib and will make it harder to draw fluid lines. As a beginner I found it helpful to draw with pencil a vertical line down the middle of the board to help me centralise my design.

Pencil on your design to your chalkboard. Have your ruler handy to mark out any straight lines where you need them. Prep your pen with paint and start drawing. Try to keep your pen moving as when you stop you will leave a thicker paint mark - as a beginner it is best to go over the work you have done with the posca pen once or twice to balance this out. Remember if you make a mistake you can correct it, and if your lines have a bit of a shake to them (nervous first tries can show) don't worry because you can always make the lines just a little bit thicker afterwards to cover this.

Once your design is complete and has dried, rub away any excess pencil markings, use a black paint pen, sharpie, or chalkboard paint to tidy up any mistakes or smudges, and remember to varnish if you intend to use your board outside.

THE CHALK SPOT TIP: If your nib gets blunt, turn it upside down.

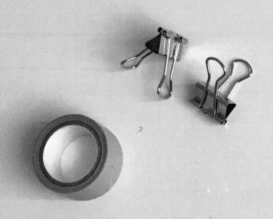

Lettering & Design

Mastering two fonts and bringing it
all together

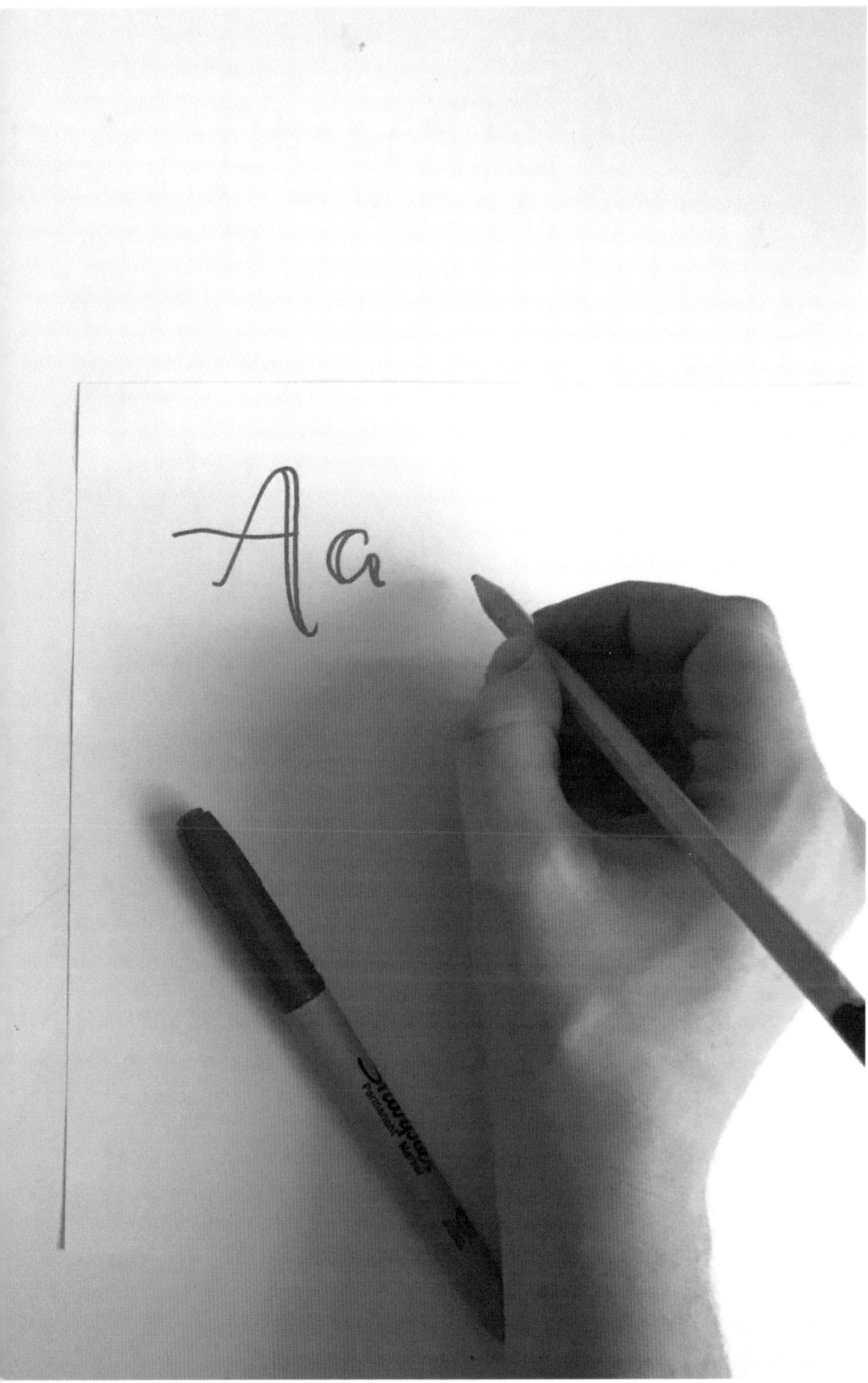
Aa
Permanent Marker

lettering
& TYPES OF FONTS

In this section we will master how to letter two fonts to use for our modern signwriting. These are modern calligraphy and a simple block text. Let's start with calligraphy.

Modern Calligraphy

Modern Calligraphy is a new term used to describe the calligraphy that is now being used widely. It is an extension of the traditional copperplate calligraphy, traditionally created with a nib and ink, but is now more fun and resembles a more natural handwriting. As we do not use a nib and ink with our signwriting, we can achieve the same style by faking it. We refer to this as faux calligraphy.

So what is faux calligraphy?

faux Calligraphy

By making sure your natural joined up handwriting has a sensible amount of space between each letter, you can achieve the elegant thick and thin lines by making the downstrokes twice as thick, and you don't need to use a calligraphy pen once!

FAUX CALLIGRAPHY STEP BY STEP

Let me show you how to achieve this with the word hello.

1 *Write your word in a flowing joined up style.*

2 *Find the parts of the letters where you naturally pull down when writing.*

3 *Create a thicker line where the downstrokes are and leave the upstrokes thin.*

4 *Fill the downstroke in.*

THE CHALK SPOT TIP:
Make sure you are sitting comfortably with your back straight.

Rotate your paper if it is easier to write like that.

CREATING
different
FAUX CALLIGRAPHY STYLES

You can change the style of your modern calligraphy by adjusting the way you fake it. If you find it difficult to join your letters up you can separate them and add the parts to join later. You can also space your lettering differently within words to create different looks. Let me show you below.

There's nothing wrong with not being able to join your handwriting up naturally. If you find it difficult to do this, and joining your letters up doesn't come easy, separate each letter as normal, and then add the parts which should join afterwards.

Join together   *Join together*

Before   **After**

As a beginner you may find it easier to control the spacing between each letter this way, as this also creates a multitude of different styles. Larger spaces between letters can create a more spidery style, whereas smaller spaces can give your letters more bounce.

Spider   *bounce*

Experimenting with different letter heights can also change the style of your lettering. Elongated l's and t's can really bring your calligraphy to life.

little

You can also create different styles depending on where you place the second line on the downstroke. Practice drawing the second line to the left and the right of the downstroke to find out which looks better for your handwriting.

Your lettering should resemble something like this ready to have the downstroke filled in.

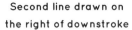

Second line drawn on the right of downstroke

Second line drawn on the left of downstroke

Remember that your style of modern calligraphy is your own, just like your natural handwriting is your own. You should find your own comfortable style to create the most natural looking calligraphy for you. Refer to the following alphabets on the next two pages.

These show faux calligraphy before and after, and in two different styles. Have a quick practice of some of the shapes they create, such as the 'o' and and the 'l'.

Please refer to the next two pages for individual letters and how they should look.

A a   B b   C c

D d   E e   F f   G g

H h   J i   J j   K k   L l

M m   N n   O o   P p   Q q

R r   S s   T t   U u

V v   W w   X x   Y y   Z z

Aa   Bb   Cc   Dd

Ee   Ff   Gg   Hh   Ii

Jj   Kk   Ll   Mm

Nn   Oo   Pp   Qq

Rr   Ss   Tt   Uu   Vv

Ww   Xx   Yy   Zz

SANS SERIF

We can also achieve a handsome bold font that will really stand out by using the same techniques as with the Calligraphy. Keep your letters tall and straight and create a thicker line at the downstroke part of each letter. Follow the steps below to achieve the look.

For example

1 *Make your lines tall and rigid, don't be afraid to extend them a bit more than it feels comfortable to*

2 *Find the parts of each letter where you drew a downstroke*

3 *Draw a double line at the downstroke, and box in at the top and the bottom.*

4 *Fill the downstroke in.*

> *THE CHALK SPOT TIP: Use a ruler to draw out with pencil where the top and the bottom of each letter should reach, as shown in this example.*

26

A   B   C

D   E   F   G

H   I   J   K   L

M   N   O   P   Q

R   S   T   U

V   W   X   Y   Z

Practice space

(or for doodles)

Worksheets

The worksheet pages give you space to practice your letters individually, with helpful guidelines to keep you on track. You do not have to stay rigidly amongst the lines however, modern calligraphy looks beautiful when it is bouncy and fun, so don't worry too much if your letters jump around. Concentrate on the shapes they each make, where the downstrokes are and how you start and finish each letter so you can get a feel for how you might join your letters together eventually.

It is important to remember that you will get the best start with mastering lettering when you practice, practice, practice. You will find it much easier to write words and sentences when you have drawn hundreds of individual letters. Your hand and brain will remember the shapes that it has practiced and will give you fluid movements when you come to writing words.

I recommend using a hard pencil with your worksheets as it will flow easier than most pens. Have fun!

A a

A

Bb

B

ℓ c

C

Dd

D

$\mathcal{E}e$

E

F f

F

Gg

G

Hh

H

Ji

I

J j

J

K k

K

L ℓ

L

M m

M

Nn

N

O o

O

$\mathcal{P}$ ρ

$\mathcal{P}$

Qq

Q

Rr

R

S s

S

$\mathcal{T}\,t$

$\mathcal{T}$

Uu

U

V v

V

Ww

W

X x

X

$\mathcal{Y}\,\mathcal{y}$

Y

Z z

Z

Bringing it all together

The great thing about modern signwriting is that you should be experimenting with your own style, and you should embrace your own individual and unique fonts by using your natural handwriting. It will become much easier once you have mastered a look that feels comfortable to you. Try to keep your letters a similar height, and be confident to put flourishes in at the start and ends of each word to add extra elegance – you can add these in at the end to make it easier.

Chalkboard designs look best when they are balanced – but not necessarily symmetrical. Try to fill your design equally, make key words bigger, and take advantage of flourishes and illustrations to complete any gaps.

Start with your words, balance out your Calligraphy text with Bold text to make your designs eye catching and interesting. After you are happy with your text, then add your decoration and illustrations.

1 PAINT　　2 PRACTICE　　3 DECORATE

THE CHALK SPOT TIP: *Practice practice practice - keep going over the alphabets and you will find your style will become more fluid*

Inspirations

you
are
loved

YOU'RE OUR
greatest
ADVENTURE

follow
your
DREAMS

Enjoy
Today

YOU ARE MY
Sunshine

WANDERLUST

Decorating

WREATHS

BANNERS

CORNERS

Flowers

These simple but beautiful flowers are easy to master and can help you to create some beautiful bouquets of flowers on your boards. Perfect for wedding decorations.

> **THE CHALK SPOT TIP**: Use coloured pens to change the look of your boards. Match these to the themes of the day for added consistency.

THE PEONIE

Step 1. Start small with E's

Step 2. Build up around the centre and continue getting bigger

THE ROSE

Step 1. Start small with C's

Step 2. Build up around the centre and continue getting bigger

THE DAISY

Perfect to fill spaces between bigger flowers

THE LEAF

For a natural look add leaves

THE VINE

Trail vines across and down the sides of boards to fill gaps. Add small flowers along your vines for that extra detail.

THE BOUQUET

Frames

If you are fortunate to get hold of an old beautiful frame to use for a welcome board, table plan, order of service for example, there are a couple of tricks to making it look beautiful.

If you've been lucky enough to find an ideal frame, and you're planning on using it as a chalkboard, you can dispose of the glass as you won't need it. If your frame needs any touch ups, don't think twice about some paint. Gold spray paints are readily available (or any colour for that matter) and you can give your frame a once over if you wish to brighten it up.

Some frames come with a wood back, which is perfect to use as a chalkboard – others may not be suitable and you will need to find a replacement. You can either cut a foam board to size, or use card for a budget friendly and easy option. If you opt for wood make sure you choose something slim so its easier to manage, try to get your measurements for cutting as precise as you can, and if your board doesn't quite fit after cutting, some sandpaper will do the trick to get it into place.

Cover your board with chalkboard paint and you will have a perfectly upcycled chalkboard ready for your faux calligraphy.

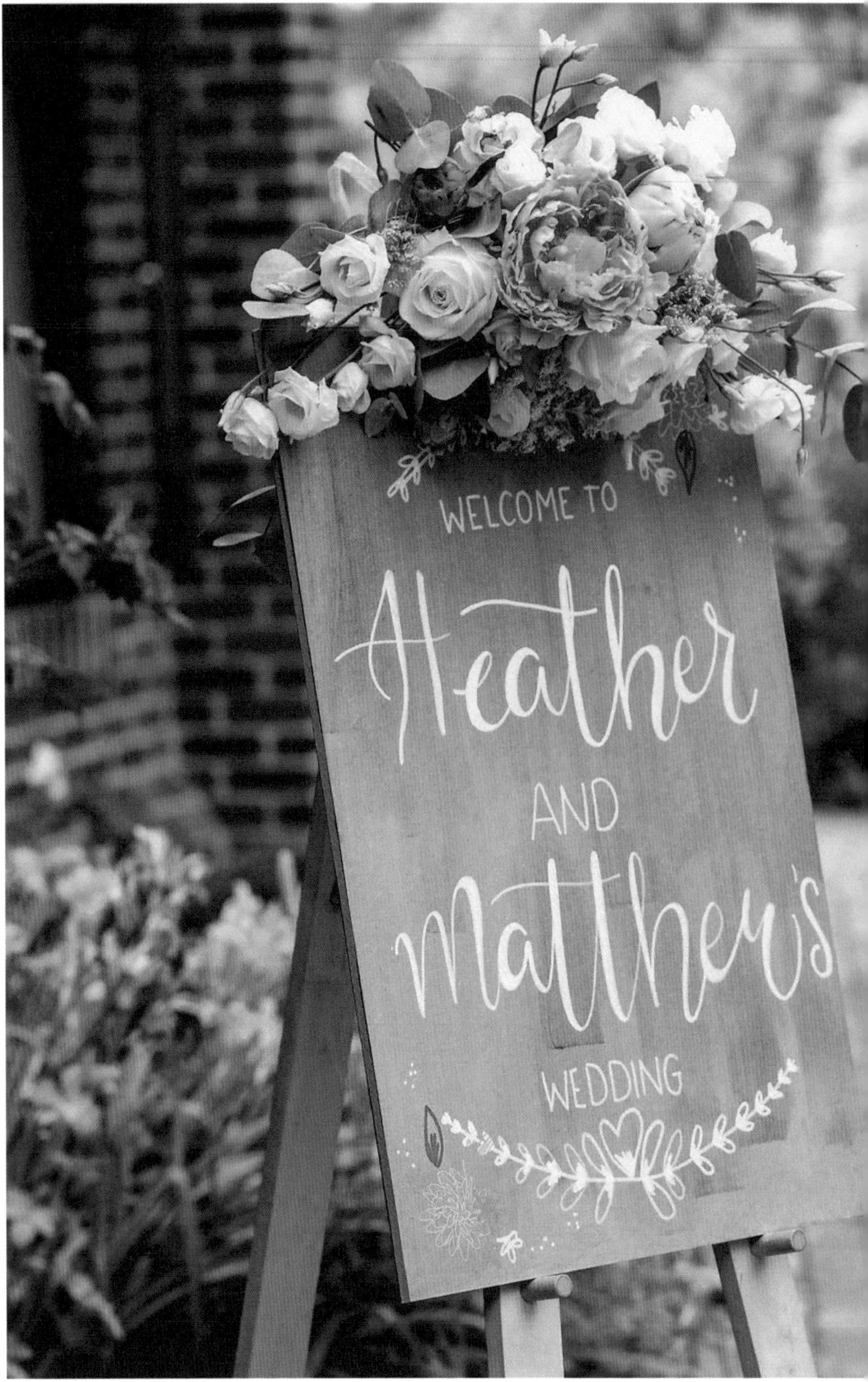
WELCOME TO
Heather
AND
Matthew's
WEDDING

Something Different
Using modern signwriting on
other surfaces

Alternative Pieces

Once you have mastered modern signwriting on chalkboards, you can then apply your new skill to lots of other surfaces. This next chapter will detail a few variations to chalkboards and how to create those pieces like I do at The Chalk Spot. These are wooden boards, glass (or perspex) and mirrors.

You can use the same recommended tools that we used on our chalkboards on these surfaces. Where changes may occur, these have been detailed in the sections following.

We are always exploring new items to put modern signwriting on. The possibilities are endless. The acrylic paint pens are great for use on almost all items, and where these may not remain permanent, the permanent sharpies are great for taking over. These can usually last a little bit longer.

WELCOME TO OUR

Best day Ever

ALL BECAUSE TWO
PEOPLE FELL IN LOVE

FROM JANUARY 2007 IN LINCOLN... MAKING MEMORIES IN...

· PARIS (FEB 2012) · VENICE (AUG 2012)

CANNES (SEPT 2011) ·

BERLIN (FEB 2013) · LONDON (DEC 2013) ·

MILAN (APR 2014) ·

· AND BARCELONA (JUL 2014) TO NAME BUT A FEW

together is a beautiful place to be

Sara & Liam

ORTON HALL HOTEL

7th AUGUST 2016

Wooden boards

Wooden boards are a great new trend, and there are loads of different types you can use. Stained MDF, wood slices and reclaimed wood are our favourites.

Reclaimed wood is a wonderful thing, readily available, and usually free. You just need to make sure you sand pieces of reclaimed wood well on the areas you wish to signwrite onto. Otherwise the acrylic paint will either seep and bleed into the wood, or you will get lumpy text from an unsmooth surface. I also recommend using a transparent sealant on the wood as well, to give extra protection for your signwriting base.

You can pick up pallets and wood from wood yards, or you might know someone who can get a pallet from work for example. Being confident to ask will go a long way if you want to save money and salvage well.

If you are after something less rustic looking, picking up some MDF from your local DIY store will do just the trick.

To make your MDF look as natural as possible, cover with a matt wood stain. Choose a shade best suited to your day, and apply sparingly with a large brush – don't worry about brush marks as these will add to your fake wood effect. Remember less is more with wood stain - you can always add more later, but you cannot remove it.

Once dry you have a beautiful base for your signwriting.

Glass & Mirrors

To really create an impact with your signwriting, have a go at using glass and mirrors. Mirrors are harder to do as you cannot use a pencil or a guide, so make sure you practice your design first and have a baby wipe handy for any mistakes. When signwriting on glass you can place your design under the glass surface to trace. If the thought of glass worries you, a great alternative is perspex.

PERSPEX

Perspex is a fantastic new trend, perfect for minimalist styles and has a modern and beautiful look to it.

Like glass, you can place a design underneath to trace. You can pick perspex up from craft stores, and it looks beautiful framed.

THINKING Outside THE BOX

Once you have the confidence to draw without pencil guides and stencils, you are free to signwrite on all manner of surfaces. I had particular fun writing on leaves and porcelain to show you how this is possible. Other ideas include wooden crates, hurricane lanterns, hangers, sweet jars... the list is endless.

The Chalk Spot blog is bursting with fresh ideas and inspiration; it is always well worth visiting.

Weddings & Events
Personalise your occasion

Once in a while, right in the middle of an Ordinary life, love gives us a fairytale

Handmade Wedding

Wedding planning can be a nightmare for some brides and grooms; but for some of us it can be the most enjoyable part of the build up. It's enjoyable when we can create handmade items and personalise our day by making our own decorations and stationary.

My favourite part of our wedding planning was making our signs and filling our marquee with frames containing quotes, stories, poems and lyrics, which were personal to us. It made our planning fun and we enjoyed reminiscing about our relationship. Having the skills to create these items made creating them fun and easy.

Upcycling old items is a beautiful way to decorate a wedding. It suits lots of themes such as Rustic and Vintage. You can also add character to Classic and Classy themes with a simple chalkboard in a gorgeous old decorative frame. There's nothing more exciting than breathing life into old items. It didn't take me long to pick up some simple upcycle skills, knowing about reclaimed wood, and discovering where to find second hand frames. It's worth getting to know your local second hand shops and wood yards.

Once you have the basics to get started, decorating your new treasured items will be easy with the hints and tips in this guide.

Having a personalised wedding is so on trend at the moment, and by making these items yourself, you can be cost effective with your planning.

I hope these additional pages can help you to enjoy your wedding planning as much as I did mine.

Welcome

Welcome signage has become big news in the event industry. You will see a welcome sign at most weddings and parties. They are my most favourite chalkboard to make, and now we do wooden versions and perspex versions as well, there is no end to the possibilities of displaying a welcome on any surface you fancy.

Designing a welcome board for a wedding is my most favourite job to do. I love to listen to couples ideas on what they might like on their board, taking note of their colour schemes and their choice of flowers. I particularly love choosing doodles and artwork to add to the board that is personal to the couple and means something to them.

Consider both portrait and landscape welcome signs, as both options can look fantastic. Portrait boards look great with lots of detail, and landscape boards look great with minimal detail. One version may suit your theme better than the other.

Take your time to practice the names, and use your pencil to mark out where they will go. The names look great in the centre of the board with large lettering. You want the names to be the main focus of the board. Once you have settled on where to pop the names, then work around them with your design (if any). Flowers are very popular and by choosing your colours carefully you can really build up some beautiful floral designs. Refer to our flowers page for inspiration if you need some.

THE CHALK SPOT TIP: Decorate your board with real flowers draped over the top.

Paul & Martina

Welcome to our Wedding

table plan

One
BRIDE & GROOM
JILL PERRY
ROGER PERRY
LOUISE MOORE
PAUL MOORE
LOLA MOORE
SCARLETT MOORE
JAY SHARP

two
VICTORIA PAYNE
DEAN PAYNE
JENNIFER JEFFREY
EDWARD PERRY
TRISH TRIGGS
JOHN TRIGGS

three
KATIE TAYLOR
ROY TAYLOR
DAVID BROOKS
ANNA BARNARD
DEREK BARNARD
GILLIAN PARRACK
ALAN PARRACK
OLIVIA ROBERTSON
HENRY ROBERTSON
ISLA ROBERTSON

four
LOUISE KITE
CHRIS KITE
MOLLY KITE
PAULINE ROY
GUS ROY
ANNE SHARMAN
GEOFF SHARMAN
HELEN BELL
HUGH BELL

five
LYNDA BUMPSTEAD
CLAIRE SHARP
ALFIE SHARP
JULIA MOORE
PETER MOORE
LYN SNELL
MAL SNELL
DOROTHY PAGE
GARY PAGE

Six
KATE FREEMAN
BEN RILEY
CHRISSY SIMMONDS
KIM SIMMONDS
REBECCA GATES
KELLY PACKHAM
KEITH PACKHAM
SCARLETT PACKHAM

Seven
JULIA DEAN
STEVE DEAN
SANDRA DEAN
GEOFF DOWN
SAM CASSIDY
DARREN CASSIDY
KERRY MCLEAN
WARREN MCLEAN
ORLA MCLEAN

eight
ALISON KELLY
MARGARET LITTLE
JULIA NYE
MIKE NYE
HELEN VERITY
JOAN GALLIGAN
EAMMON GALLIGAN
JANE PHILLIPS
KEN PHILLIPS

Table Plans
AND NUMBERS

Table numbers can be styled in so many ways. Use the table numbers in frames, on postcards or attached to sticks to place in your table centre flowers.

You can also display a table plan to help guests find their seats. Simple designs are key so they are easy to read. Make sure you practice a layout on paper first. Knowing how big your handwriting is and how many tables to put on each section of your plan will help you plot it all out. I always use a ruler with a table plan. I draw a small spot where i would like each table number to go, then freehand the lists of names below each number. You may like to draw pencil lines for your names to keep it neat and tidy.

1 2 3 4 5 6 7 8 9 0

one two three

four five six

seven eight

nine ten

Stationery

You can apply your faux calligraphy to your stationery items for a handmade feel that is personal to you and for your guests. Examples include menu cards, invitations, and orders of service.

You may wish to create each of your stationery items by hand, alternatively you can upload your designs onto a computer to print out in bulk. You could just hand letter a few choice words, such as mr & mrs, and use computer fonts for all the other details for a handmade but neat and modern design

---

Favours

If you have time to make your own favours, these can also be personalised with faux calligraphy. You could use leaves, pebbles, labels for jam jars - there are so many options, and most of these can double up as place names to save you time and money.

THE CHALK SPOT TIP: *Try coloured and / or metallic gel pens to create different looks.*

FINISHING
Touches

Once you've created your beautiful decorations, they need somewhere equally beautiful to be displayed. Easels can be bought cheaply on the Internet, or you might find the venue have them to borrow. Paint them with chalk paint to create a different look. You could hang with rope by drilling holes near the top. Your local DIY store will have lots of different ropes to choose from.

Try ladders and hampers, boxes and crates to build up display corners and pop your finished items nearby. Have fun, be creative, and enjoy it.

I hope you have enjoyed your guide to Modern Signwriting.

Please send us images of your hard work, we love to see how you are getting on. Please use #thechalkspot to help us find your images on social media.

For inspiration and ideas please refer to our blog, our galleries on the website, and keep up to date with our social media pages.

Acknowledgements

This guide would not have come about had it not been for some very supporting friends and family. Despite my husband Dan telling me that people want to see how I do what I do, I wasn't really listening. The turning point came at a wedding fair when Clair from Creative Brides encouraged me to get a table out and make my wedding boards on display (I was going to hide behind a curtain, too shy to show off). It's not usual to order a bespoke item at a wedding fair then get to take it home on the same day. To watch your bespoke item be made was certainly not something I had ever experienced before, so I was nervous about doing it. It was, however, a huge success. Thank you Clair.

The biggest encouragement I had came from Fiona who runs a beautiful floristry business Anemone Blue. Fiona, thank you for asking me to host a chalkboard class. You forced me to think about how I could teach what I know, and create something nobody else was doing. Without these experiences I would not have been brave enough to give up my secrets.

Without my timeless friend Erika I would not have been able to put it onto paper. Erika, your patience and wonderful knowledge has brought all my thoughts and images together. I really do love our teamwork.

Thank you Dad and Becca for helping me understand what it needs to say. Thank you Sarah for being perfect with words, this little guide would not read quite as wonderfully as it does now had you not given it some love and care. Last but not least, thank you Mum for giving me time.